FUN FACT FILE: BUGS!

20 FUN FACTS ABOUT PRAYING MANTISES

By Adrienne Houk Maley

Please visit our website, www.garethstevens.com. For a free color catalog of all our high-quality books, call toll free 1-800-542-2595 or fax 1-877-542-2596.

Library of Congress Cataloging-in-Publication Data

Maley, Adrienne Houk
      20 fun facts about praying mantises / by Adrienne Houk Maley.
p.   cm. – (Fun fact file: bugs!)
Includes bibliographical references and index.
Summary: This book describes praying mantises, including their physical characteristics, habitats, and eating habits.
Contents: Nature's Kung Fu masters – Mantis bodies – I've got my eyes on you – Who's in the hood? – Praying for prey – Hungry bugs – Listen up! – Fancy protection – The case of the praying mantis – Checkmate – Great gardeners – Magnificent mantis meals – Close encounters.
ISBN 978-1-4339-8240-8 (hard bound)
ISBN 978-1-4339-8241-5 (pbk.)
ISBN 978-1-4339-8242-2 (6-pack)
      1. Praying mantis—Juvenile literature   [1. Praying mantis]
I. Title 2013
595.7/27—dc23

First Edition

Published in 2013 by
Gareth Stevens Publishing
111 East 14th Street, Suite 349
New York, NY 10003

Designer: Sarah Liddell
Editor: Greg Roza

Photo credits: Cover, p. 1 Image Focus/Shutterstock.com; pp. 4, 7 (left), 8 Eric Isselee/Shutterstock.com; p. 5 (large mantis) GIRODJL/Shutterstock.com; p. 5 (small mantis) GK Hart/Vikki Hart/Photodisc/Getty Images; p. 6 Jens Stolt/Shutterstock.com; p. 7 (right) © iStockphoto.com/muratseyit; p. 9 Katarina Christenson/Shutterstock.com; pp. 10, 14, 20, 22 Cathy Keifer/Shutterstock.com; p. 11 (mantis) Florian Andronache/Shutterstock.com; p. 11 (cockroach) © iStockphoto.com/Atelopus; pp. 12, 13 iStockphoto/Thinkstock.com; p. 15 Alexander Chelmdeev/Shutterstock.com; p. 16 sarah2/Shutterstock.com; p. 17 Visuals Unlimited, Inc./Robert Pickett/Visuals Unlimited/Getty Images; p. 18 phittavas/Shutterstock.com; p. 19 nico99/Shutterstock.com; p. 21 © iStockphoto.com/aetmeister; p. 23 kevin connors/Shutterstock.com; p. 24 Emily Goodwin/Shutterstock.com; p. 25 © iStockphoto.com/135133; p. 26 nico99/Shutterstock.com; p. 27 (cricket) pale62/Shutterstock.com; p. 27 (praying mantis and spider) Kristy Pargeter/Shutterstock.com; p. 27 (grasshopper, mouse, and hummingbird) Nebojsa S/Shutterstock.com; p. 27 (frog) Potapov Alexander/Shutterstock.com; p. 29 Dobermaraner/Shutterstock.com.

Printed in the United States of America

CPSIA compliance information: Batch #CW13GS: For further information contact Gareth Stevens, New York, New York at 1-800-542-2595.

Contents

Words in the glossary appear in **bold** type the first time they are used in the text.

Nature's Kung Fu Masters

Some people love praying mantises more than other insects because of their supercool looks. However, they can be hard to spot because they blend in so well with their surroundings.

Many people think praying mantises look cool because they hold their front legs as if they're praying—or like they're about to do kung fu! Maybe that's why other bugs stay far away. This position allows praying mantises to be ready for a quick attack on their **prey**.

Depending on the species, or kind, an adult praying mantis can be 0.5 to 6 inches (1.3 to 15.2 cm) long.

FACT 1

A praying mantis's front legs are strong enough to crush some prey.

A praying mantis's front legs can strike in 1/20 of a second. These strong, spiny legs can easily hold on to struggling prey. A praying mantis can easily crush a grasshopper or cricket with its front legs.

This praying mantis holds its prey tightly in its forelegs and eats it alive.

A female mantis has a longer, heavier body than a male and shorter wings.

female mantis

male mantis

Male mantises can fly, but females usually can't.

A mantis has two large outer wings that protect two smaller inner wings. A male's wings are longer than a female's wings. Males can fly short distances to get away from **predators**. Female mantises are heavier. They jump and crawl, but they usually can't fly.

I've Got My Eyes on You

FACT 3

Praying mantises have two kinds of eyes.

A praying mantis's large eyes are positioned on the sides of its triangular-shaped head. They're very good at seeing everything around them, especially movement. Praying mantises also have three simple eyes between their two large eyes. These smaller eyes only sense light.

Praying mantises can turn their head side to side, allowing them to see nearly all the way around them.

8

The compound eye of the praying mantis has thousands of light-sensitive parts.

FACT 4

Praying mantises see much better than many insects.

The praying mantis's large eyes are **compound eyes**. They can detect quick movements and see objects as far as 50 feet (15 m) away. Flies have compound eyes, too, but many can only see objects clearly a few millimeters away.

Who's in the Hood?

FACT 5

There are more than 2,000 species of mantises all over the world.

Praying mantises can be found in many warm regions around the world. They're also found in cooler parts of North America and Europe. The California mantis is the only species that's native to the United States.

The Chinese praying mantis was originally brought to the United States to hunt insects that ruined farm crops.

The praying mantis is a close relative of the cockroach.

Mantises are part of the Dictyoptera (DIHK-tee-ahp-tuh-ruh) order of insects. This word comes from the ancient Greek words for "net" and "wing." Cockroaches are also members of this order. Mantises and cockroaches have leathery wings and chewing mouthparts.

cockroach

FACT 7

The praying mantis has a flexible neck and body.

The praying mantis is very **flexible**. It can turn its head 180 degrees. This is an **adaptation** that helps the praying mantis locate and follow its prey. Just before it attacks, it sways its body back and forth.

Swaying may help a praying mantis judge how far to jump to get its prey. Or, it may help the bug hide among leaves moving in the wind.

FACT 8

A praying mantis isn't praying. It's waiting for a meal to pass by.

Like many other predators, the praying mantis **ambushes** its prey. The praying mantis's large, bent front legs look like a person praying. However, these arms are just waiting to spring out and grab a meal. The forelegs have spines to help hold wiggling prey in place.

Hungry Bugs

FACT 9

Praying mantises chew their food well.

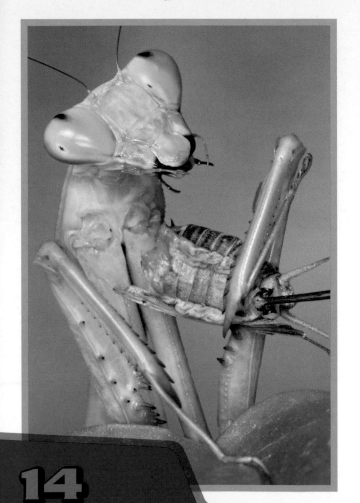

Certain insects, such as mosquitoes, butterflies, and honeybees, use mouthparts to suck up their food. Not praying mantises. They move their jaws sideways to chew live prey. They eat quickly, often leaving just a few limbs behind.

This giant Asian mantis is eating a cricket.

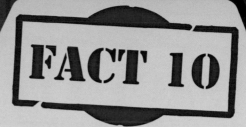

FACT 10

Praying mantises sometimes kill and eat larger animals.

Praying mantises aren't picky eaters. They eat almost any kind of insect. These predators creep up slowly on prey and then attack. They sometimes hunt small mice, frogs, lizards, hummingbirds, and even snakes.

The lightning-quick speed of a praying mantis helps it capture all sorts of prey.

FACT 11

A praying mantis's ear isn't on its head.

The praying mantis has an ear in the middle of its **abdomen**. This ear helps the praying mantis detect sound waves that bats use to catch prey. When it hears the sounds, the praying mantis dives out of the way of the hungry bat.

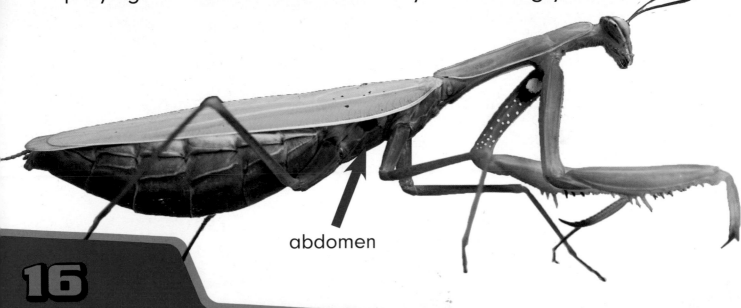

abdomen

Praying mantises are acrobats.

Once the praying mantis hears a bat, it takes off. It gets out of the way by opening its wings and diving down. Scientists have found that the louder a bat's signal, the more moves the praying mantis makes while fleeing.

Bats are a major predator of praying mantises.

Fancy Protection

A praying mantis's color allows it to hide in plain sight. Some can even change color.

Green meadows are a great place for green praying mantises to hide. The damper the air is, the greener the mantis will appear. The ghost mantis looks like a dried-up leaf. The orchid mantis has legs that look like pink flowers.

The orchid mantis looks much like the blossoms of the plant it's named after.

Praying mantises make themselves look larger to scare away enemies.

When a praying mantis is in trouble, it may stand tall and spread out its wings. Some have brightly colored wings that tell enemies to stay away. They also make hissing sounds, open their mouths, and grab with their front legs.

The Case of the Praying Mantis

FACT 15

Depending on the species, female praying mantises lay 10 to 400 eggs at one time.

In fall, female praying mantises lay eggs in foamy masses close to the ground. The foam hardens and forms cases called oothecae (oh-uh-THEE-kee). They're almost impossible to find. This protects the many tiny praying mantises, called nymphs, growing inside.

An egg case is strong enough to survive the winter. Here, tiny nymphs come out of an egg case in late spring.

These mantis nymphs haven't grown wings yet.

FACT 16

Baby praying mantises get their good looks from their parents.

Nymphs all emerge from the egg case at about the same time. They look like a small copy of their mom and dad. Nymphs don't have wings yet, but will grow them during their last **molt**.

FACT 17

Praying mantises molt six to nine times before reaching adult size.

As the mantis grows, it sheds its **exoskeleton** several times, or molts. Once it gets too big for its outer skin, it stretches, splits its skin, and slowly wiggles out of it. The mantis hangs upside down while its new exoskeleton hardens.

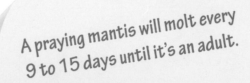

A praying mantis will molt every 9 to 15 days until it's an adult.

Checkmate

Female praying mantises sometimes eat the head of their mate.

While **mating**, female praying mantises may eat some or all of their mate's head! Scientists aren't sure why. They might need the **nutrients** for their young. However, some scientists think **captive** females become angry, causing them to eat their mates.

Great Gardeners

Praying mantises are great gardeners.

Praying mantises eat just about any insect. Because of this, they're great for garden pest control. If you see one in the garden, leave it alone so it can protect your plants by eating harmful pests, such as grasshoppers and beetles.

Some gardeners order oothecae online and receive them in the mail. Once the nymphs hatch, they help keep the garden pest-free.

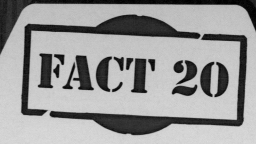

Praying mantises often eat each other.

If you want more mantises in the garden, avoid using pesticides, which are substances used to kill bugs. Unfortunately, it can be hard to keep praying mantises in a garden because they're cannibalistic. That means they eat each other!

The brown mantis in this photograph is having a green mantis for dinner!

Magnificent Mantis Meals

Praying mantises are hungry insects, and they eat a lot! The size of the meal doesn't matter, since larger praying mantises have been known to hunt snakes up to about 20 inches (50 cm) long. The bar graph on page 27 lists several of their favorite meals, although they eat much more.

small
praying mantis

spider

cricket

grasshopper

frog

mouse

hummingbird

large
praying mantis

centimeters

2 2 2 5 7 8 9 12

Close Encounters

Praying mantises prefer to live in warmer climates around the world. Only 20 kinds live in North America, while Africa has 880 known species. They blend in with their surroundings so well that they're hard to see no matter where in the world you are.

If you're lucky enough to come across a praying mantis, take the time to observe its weird body features and habits. Many people even think that praying mantises look like aliens from another world!

Praying mantises can be kept as pets as long as you feed them live food, usually lots of crickets.

29

Glossary

abdomen: the part of an insect's body that contains the stomach

adaptation: a change in a type of animal that happens over time and makes it better able to live in its surroundings

ambush: to attack from a hiding place

captive: the state of being caged

compound eye: an eye made up of many separate seeing parts

exoskeleton: the hard outer covering of an animal's body

flexible: able to bend easily

mate: to come together to make babies. Also, one of two animals that come together to produce babies.

molt: the act of shedding an exoskeleton that has become too small

nutrient: something a living thing needs to grow and stay alive

predator: an animal that hunts other animals for food

prey: an animal that is hunted by other animals for food

For More Information

Books

Goldish, Meish. *Deadly Praying Mantises.* New York, NY: Bearport Publishing, 2008.

Markle, Sandra. *Praying Mantises: Hungry Insect Heroes.* Minneapolis, MN: Lerner Publications, 2008.

Websites

Praying Mantis

www.environmentalgraffiti.com/animals/news-praying-mantis
Read more about praying mantises and see amazing photographs of them up close.

The Praying Mantis

www.theprayingmantis.org
Learn much more about praying mantises on this site dedicated to the insect.

Praying Mantis vs. Hummingbird

www.environmentalgraffiti.com/featured/praying-mantis-vs-hummingbird/20203
See amazing photographs and videos of praying mantises hunting for—and eating—hummingbirds.

Publisher's note to educators and parents: Our editors have carefully reviewed these websites to ensure that they are suitable for students. Many websites change frequently, however, and we cannot guarantee that a site's future contents will continue to meet our high standards of quality and educational value. Be advised that students should be closely supervised whenever they access the Internet.

Index